RISE, HEAL AND LEAD

A 21-Day Devotional for Women Called to Rise in Faith, Heal the Heart and Lead With God-Given Purpose

RISE, HEAL AND LEAD

A 21-Day Devotional for Women Called to Rise in Faith, Heal the Heart and Lead With God-Given Purpose

DR. CAROLYN COLEMAN
THE LADY OF WISDOM

The Lady of Wisdom Publishing Company

Published by The Lady of Wisdom Publishing Company April 24, 2026.

ISBN: 978-1-966970-06-4 (paperback)
ISBN: 978-1-966970-07-1 (eBook)

LCCN: 2025924625

Cover Designed by The Lady of Wisdom Creative Studio

Formatted by Written Words Publishing LLC

Printed in the United States of America

First Edition

DEDICATION

This book is lovingly dedicated:

To the women who carry vision in their spirit and courage in their steps.

To every daughter who has heard the quiet whisper of God calling her to rise.

May these pages remind you that your voice matters, your presence matters, and your leadership is needed.

Rise with grace.
Lead with wisdom.

LETTER TO MY DAUGHTER, NICHOLE

My Beloved Daughter,

Before this devotional ever became a manuscript, it lived first as prayer. Many of the reflections that now fill these pages were whispered to God during seasons of learning, waiting, healing, and rising. Through those seasons, I often found myself thinking of you.

A mama's heart carries many prayers, but one of the deepest is the desire that her child will know who she is in God; not simply by what the world says, or by what circumstances try to define, but by the steady voice of truth that reminds her she is chosen, capable, and covered by grace.

Nichole, you have always carried a quiet strength. It is the kind of strength that does not need to announce itself, yet it sustains, uplifts, and endures. Watching you grow into your calling has been one of the great privileges of my life.

This devotional was written not only for the women who will read it, but also for you. For the woman you are, the woman you are growing into, and the woman God continues to shape through every season of life. My prayer is that these words remind you, and every reader who turns these pages, that rising is not about perfection. Rising is about trusting God with each step forward.

There will be moments in life when the road feels uncertain, when strength feels distant, or when the weight of responsibility seems heavier than expected. In those moments, remember this: the same God who calls you is the God who sustains you.

Rise with courage.

Heal with grace.

Lead with wisdom.

You are never alone on this journey. My prayers walk with you, and God's presence goes before you.

With love, pride, and unending faith in the woman God created you to be,

Mama
Dr. Carolyn Coleman
The Lady of Wisdom

Letter to Amiel

My Precious Amiel,

By the time you read these words, you will already know that you are deeply loved. Love surrounds you in the prayers spoken over your life, the hands that guide you, and the faith that has been planted in your heart.

This devotional was written during a season of reflection and rising. While many women will read these pages, I also wrote them with the generations of our family in mind, especially you.

You are growing up in a world that will try to tell you many things about who you should be. Some voices will be loud, and some may try to make you doubt your worth. But always remember this truth: your identity does not come from the world around you. Your identity comes from the God who created you.

You were created with purpose.

You were created with wisdom.

You were created with strength.

As you grow, there will be moments when life feels confusing or uncertain. That is part of learning and becoming strong. When those moments come, take a breath, pray, and remember that God walks beside you every step of the way.

Never be afraid to ask questions. Never be afraid to seek wisdom. And never believe that your voice or your dreams are too small to matter.

My prayer for you is simple but powerful: that you grow into a young woman who rises with courage, heals with grace, and leads with kindness and wisdom.

Always remember that your family stands behind you, and God's love surrounds you.

With all my love,

Nana

Dr. Carolyn Coleman

The Lady of Wisdom

A Sacred Pause

Before you begin this journey, take a moment to breathe. This devotional was not written for perfection. It was written for real life. For the seasons of joy and the seasons of healing, the moments of strength, and the moments when faith must carry you forward.

Perhaps you are opening these pages in a time of clarity. Perhaps you are opening them while carrying questions, burdens, or quiet grief. Wherever you find yourself today, you are welcome here.

This journey is not about rushing toward change. It is about walking gently with God, one day, one prayer, and one rising step at a time.

Over the next twenty-one days, allow yourself to be honest. Allow yourself to listen. Allow yourself to grow. And most of all, allow yourself to rise.

Take a deep breath. Whisper a prayer. Then turn the page. Your rising begins now.

"Arise, shine;
for your light has come,
and the glory of the LORD rises upon you"
(Isaiah 60:1).

OPENING LITANY

THE DECLARATION OF RISING

Permission Granted

Beloved, you don't need another sign.
You don't need another confirmation.
You don't need approval from anyone but God.
This is your moment to say:

"I give myself permission to rise."

Not later.
Not someday.
Now.
This is your new beginning and you own it.

The Declaration of Rising

I give myself permission to be new.
I give myself permission to heal.
I give myself permission to grow.
I give myself permission to arrive fully in my now.

I am rising: boldly, beautifully, and unapologetically.
And nothing can stop the woman I am rising into.

THE RISING MANIFESTO

I am done shrinking.
I am done apologizing for my light.
I am done carrying weight that is not mine.
I am done living small in spaces God made big for me.

I embrace wisdom.
I embrace healing.
I embrace clarity.
I embrace my voice.
I embrace my calling.

I am stepping into my new now.
I am choosing myself with grace.
I am honoring who I am rising into.

This is my season of permission.
My season of ownership.
My season of becoming.

21-Day Ownership Prayer

Father,

Thank You for calling me into my new now.
Thank You for the strength to let go,
the courage to rise, and the wisdom to walk
in who You created me to be.

For the next 21 days:
Align my thoughts with Your truth.
Align my heart with Your peace.
Align my steps with Your purpose
Align my identity with Heaven's vision for me.

I take ownership of my becoming.
Not by perfection, but by surrender.
Not by striving, but by grace.
Not by fear, but by faith.

I receive my new now.
Amen.

The New Now Creed

I am not waiting.
I am not hesitating.
I am not retreating.

I step into my new now with:
Authority.
Identity.
Wisdom.
Courage.
Grace.

I honor my healing.
I honor my growth.
I honor my transformation.

I own my voice.
I own my worth.
I own my rising.

This is my new now and I rise.

TABLE OF CONTENTS

Author's Note

Writing Rise Heal and Lead has been both a spiritual journey and a personal reflection on the many seasons that shape our lives. These pages were not written from theory alone, but from prayer, experience, and the lessons God continues to teach me about faith, healing, and perseverance.

Like many of you, my life has held moments of great joy as well as seasons of loss and challenge. Through each experience, I have witnessed the faithfulness of God guiding, strengthening, and restoring what seemed impossible to mend. This devotional was written with that same hope in mind. Wherever you find yourself today, you will be reminded that rising is always possible with God.

My desire is that these reflections encourage you to walk forward with courage, to allow healing to take place in the hidden places of your heart, and to lead your life

with wisdom and grace. Spiritual growth rarely happens in dramatic moments alone; it is often found in the quiet daily choices to trust God, to forgive, to begin again, and to keep moving forward.

If these words have encouraged you even in a small way, then the purpose of this book has been fulfilled. May you continue to rise, heal, and lead with faith, knowing that God's presence walks with you every step of the journey.

With gratitude and encouragement,

Dr. Carolyn Coleman
The Lady of Wisdom

INTRODUCTION

The Call to Rise

There are moments when the soul senses a quiet call, a holy stirring deep within, a knowing that you were made for more than survival. There comes a time when what once held you can no longer define you, and what once wounded you can no longer rule you. Something within begins to awaken and rise.

Rise, Heal and Lead is a 21-day devotional journey designed to help women rediscover clarity, courage, and spiritual alignment. Through scripture, reflection, prayer, and daily affirmations, you are guided into deeper faith, emotional renewal, and confident leadership.

This journey calls you to awaken your spiritual identity and remember who you are in God. It leads you to release burdens that no longer belong to you and lay down the weight of past pain, fear, and limitation. It

strengthens your trust in God's direction, even when the path ahead is not fully visible. It invites you to embrace vision, healing, and purpose with clarity and boldness.

With wisdom, compassion, and spiritual insight, Dr. Carolyn Coleman, The Lady of Wisdom, offers a pathway for women who are ready to step forward in faith and lead with strength. Whether read privately, shared with friends, or used in church groups, this devotional invites you to embrace the next chapter of your journey.

Your story is not finished. It is time to rise.

This is not merely a devotional for reading. It is an invitation to transformation. It is a call to come out of fear, silence, delay, and spiritual fatigue. It is a summons to remember your voice, reclaim your authority, and move forward with holy confidence.

There are seasons in life that leave women carrying more than they were meant to bear. Disappointment, grief, rejection, transition, and quiet battles of the heart can weigh heavily on the soul. Yet even in those places, God still calls His daughters forward. He still strengthens, restores, and speaks life where weariness once tried to settle.

These pages are designed to help you pause long enough to hear that call again, breathe again, believe again, and rise again.

Not as a woman pretending to be whole, but as a woman allowing God to heal her from the inside out.

Not as a woman chasing titles, but as a woman embracing purpose.

Not as a woman driven by pressure, but as a woman led by presence.

As you walk through this journey, remain honest, prayerful, and open. Let the Scriptures anchor you. Let the reflections search you. Let the prayers steady you. Let the affirmations remind you that your identity is not in what broke you, but in the God who is restoring you.

You are not behind.
You are not forgotten.
You are not disqualified by what you have endured.

There is still vision in you.
There is still healing for you.
There is still leadership in you.

The hand of God is still upon your life.

This is your time to **rise** with wisdom.
This is your time to **heal** with intention.
This is your time to **lead** with faith, grace, and strength.

How to Use This Devotional

A 21-Day Rising Pathway

This is not a book you rush through. This is a journey you **walk out**.

For the next 21 days, you are not chasing perfection. You are choosing **alignment**. You are building spiritual rhythm, emotional clarity, and daily momentum. Some days will feel strong. Other days will feel tender. Keep going. **Rising is not about how you feel. It's about what you refuse to surrender.**

This devotional is designed to meet you where you are while calling you forward into who you are becoming. It requires your presence, your honesty, and your willingness to engage each day with intention.

Do not approach these pages casually. Approach them prayerfully. Set aside a consistent time each day,

even if it is only a few moments. Protect that time. Honor that space. This is where transformation takes root.

You must give yourself permission to slow down, reflect, listen, and respond. This is not about information. This is about formation.

Your Daily Rising Flow (10–20 minutes)

Each day follows the same pattern. Let the structure carry you. Do not skip ahead. Do not rush through. Allow each step to do its work within you.

1. **Read the Key Scripture**
   Read it slowly. Read it again. Let one phrase rise to your attention. Sit with it until it speaks to your spirit.

2. **Engage the Devotional Reflection**
   Read with openness. Allow the words to challenge, affirm, and stretch you. Do not just read. Receive.

3. **Respond to the Guided Prompts**
   These are not optional. This is where clarity is formed. Write honestly. Do not filter your truth.

4. **Speak the Daily Declaration**
   Your words matter. Speak with intention. Speak with authority. Speak until your spirit aligns with what you are declaring.

5. **Pray the Prayer**
   Do not rush through it. Personalize it. Let it become your conversation with God.

6. **Activate the Rising Practice**

   Faith requires movement. Apply what you have received. Even one intentional action creates momentum.

7. **Affirm and Close the Day**

   End with agreement. Reinforce what God is building within you. Carry it with you throughout your day.

You will not complete this journey the same way you started it. If you remain consistent, you will think differently, respond differently, and see yourself differently. What once felt heavy will begin to lift. What once felt unclear will begin to align.

Stay with the process. Do not measure your progress by perfection. Measure it by your willingness to return each day. This is your rising season.

Three Rules That Protect Your Progress

1) **No shame.**

   If you miss a day, don't quit. Don't restart. **Continue.** The goal is completion, not perfection.

2) **One page at a time.**

   Don't read ahead when you're avoiding conviction. Let each day do its work.

3) **Rising requires support.**
   If a prompt uncovers deep pain, do not carry it alone. Speak to a trusted friend, pastor, counselor, or mentor. Wisdom does not isolate.

Weekly Rhythm (Optional but Powerful)

At the end of **Days 7, 14, and 21**, pause and reflect:

- What has shifted in my thinking?
- What has softened in my heart?
- What has strengthened in my spirit?
- What is God asking me to release next?

For Families, Teens, and Groups

This devotional was designed to move beyond the individual reader.

- If you are a parent or leader, use **Appendix C** to start conversations that protect and strengthen your household.
- If you are walking with a teen, read **Appendix B** together and help them identify **three safe people** they can talk to.
- If you lead a ministry or group, use **Appendix D** to turn this book into a workshop and build a rising culture.

Your 21-Day Commitment

Before you begin, write your name and your start date:

Name: _______________________________________

Start Date: ____________________________________

My Rising Intentions:

____

____

____

____

My Healing Components:

____

____

____

____

My Leading Expositions:

____

____

____

____

Beloved, you don't need permission to rise.
You need ownership.

This is your new now and you rise.

PRAYER OF ALIGNMENT

Father, As I begin this twenty-one-day journey, align my heart with Your truth and my steps with Your wisdom.

Give me courage to face what needs healing, humility to receive what You are teaching, and strength to continue rising even when the process feels slow.

Let every word in these pages lead me closer to Your presence and deeper into the life You designed for me.

I surrender this journey to You. Amen.

Section I

I Rise

DAY 1: THE BEGINNING

I Rise Into New Beginnings

"He who began a good work in you will complete it…"
(Philippians 1:6 NKJV).

Devotional Reading

Every sacred journey begins with a whisper. A gentle stirring that says, "It is time." Not time to rush. Not time to prove. But time to begin with grace-filled courage.

God begins what He intends to complete. When something stirs within you (an idea, a healing, a step of faith), it is rarely random. It is often the beginning of divine movement.

Rising begins when you trust that small beginnings matter.

Meditation Prompt

What is beginning in me today?

Journal Reflections

What part of your life is longing for a new beginning?
What is God inviting you to say yes to today?
Where is the Spirit whispering, "Start here"?

Journaling Space

____

____

____

____

____

____

____

I Rise Declaration

Today, I begin with courage and surrender.
I rise in wisdom, I rise in purpose,
and I rise in the strength of God.

Prayer

Lord, thank You for new beginnings.
Give me courage to step forward in faith. Amen.

I Rise Practice

Take one small step toward something God has placed
on your heart. Write it, affirm it and walk it out.

____

____

____

____

____

____

____

____

I Rise Affirmation

I rise boldly into the new beginning
God has prepared for me.

DAY 2: THE UNVEILING

I Rise Rooted in His Presence

*"And we all, who with unveiled faces contemplate the
Lord's glory, are being transformed into his image…"*
(2 Corinthians 3:18 NIV).

Devotional Reading

Transformation begins with unveiling. God gently removes the layers that hide our true identity, our fear, comparison, insecurity, and the pressure to perform. Unveiling is not exposure. It is revelation. As each layer falls away, you begin to see yourself more clearly through God's eyes.

Meditation Prompt

What is God gently unveiling in my life?

Journal Reflections

What beliefs am I being invited to release?
What truth about my identity is emerging?
What false label must I remove?

Journaling Space

____

____

____

____

____

____

____

I Rise Declaration

I welcome divine clarity. I rise in wisdom, I rise in
purpose, and I rise in the strength of God.

Prayer

Lord, reveal who You created me to be.
Remove every false identity. Amen.

I Rise Practice

Let go of something that reflects a past season.

I Rise Affirmation

**I rise unveiled and confident in the
identity God has given me.**

DAY 3: THE AWAKENING

I Rise Still Enough to Hear

"Arise, shine; for your light has come..."
(Isaiah 60:1 NIV).

Devotional Reading

Awakening is the moment when the soul remembers its calling. You begin to see differently. You recognize possibilities you once overlooked. Awakening is not loud. It is luminous. It is the quiet realization that something within you is ready to rise again.

Meditation Prompt

Where is God awakening something new within me?

Journal Reflections

What dream or purpose is resurfacing?
What truth about myself am I rediscovering?
Where do I sense new spiritual awareness?

Journaling Space

____

____

____

____

____

____

I Rise Declaration

Rising is my assignment, wisdom is my gift,
and resting in God is my inheritance.

Prayer

Lord, awaken in me what has slept too long. Let Your
light rise upon me and guide my becoming. Amen.

I Rise Practice

Write what God is awakening in you today.

____

____

____

____

____

____

____

____

____

____

____

____

I Rise Affirmation

**I rise awake, alive, and aligned
with God's glory.**

DAY 4: THE STILLNESS

I Rise in Surrender

"Be still, and know that I am God"
(Psalm 46:10 NKJV).

Devotional Reading

Stillness is the sanctuary where God speaks the loudest. Not in the rush. Not in the noise. But in the quiet places where your heart settles and your breath slows.

Stillness is not the absence of movement. It is the presence of God. It is the holy pause where clarity finds you and peace meets you.

In stillness, God lifts burdens you did not know you were carrying and restores strength you thought you lost. Be gentle with yourself today. Let stillness renew you.

Meditation Prompt

Where in my life is God inviting me to be still?

Journal Reflections

What thoughts rise when you slow down?
What anxieties loosen their grip in silence?
What does God's presence feel like in stillness?

Journaling Space

____

____

____

____

____

____

____

I Rise Declaration

I choose stillness. I choose presence.
Rising is my assignment, wisdom is my gift,
and resting in God is my inheritance.

Prayer

Lord, quiet my spirit. Slow my mind. Let me meet You
in the stillness and be restored. Amen.

I Rise Practice

Take five minutes today to sit in silence. No
distractions, no noise. Simply breathe and be.
What did the silence speak to you?

____

____

____

____

____

____

____

____

____

I Rise Affirmation

**I rise centered, calm, and anchored
in God's stillness.**

DAY 5: THE SURRENDER

I Rise Spirit-Led

"Trust in the LORD with all your heart and lean not on your own understanding" (Proverbs 3:5 NIV).

Devotional Reading

Surrender is not giving up. It is giving over. It is the holy release where your will meets God's wisdom.

There are places where you have carried the weight too long, places where your understanding has tried to do the work of God's sovereignty.

Surrender is the moment you unclench your hands and let God hold what was never meant to exhaust you. In surrender, strength returns. Peace rises. Alignment comes. Surrender is where rising deepens.

Meditation Prompt

What am I being invited to surrender today?

Journal Reflections

What are you trying to control that
is draining your spirit?
What would happen if you released it to God?
Where do you feel resistance and where
do you feel relief?

Journaling Space

____

____

____

____

____

____

____

I Rise Declaration

I surrender what I cannot carry.
Rising is my assignment, wisdom is my gift,
and resting in God is my inheritance.

Prayer

Lord, I release my need to understand everything. I trust Your leading. I yield my will to Yours. Amen.

I Rise Practice

Write one thing you are surrendering today. Speak it aloud, then let it go.

____

____

____

____

____

____

____

____

____

I Rise Affirmation

I rise surrendered, strengthened, and safely held in God.

Day 6: The Confidence

I Rise Secure in Identity

"For the LORD will be your confidence and will keep your foot from being caught" (Proverbs 3:26 NKJV).

Devotional Reading

Confidence in God is not arrogance. It is alignment. It is the holy boldness that rises when you finally believe what God has spoken over you.

Confidence comes when Heaven's truth becomes louder than your old insecurities. When the whispers of doubt lose their authority. When you stop shrinking to make others comfortable.

Confidence is not a personality trait. It is a spiritual posture. It is standing tall in who God says you are, even when your feelings have not caught up.

Today, let confidence rise in you like morning light.

Meditation Prompt

Where is God inviting me to stand
in holy confidence today?

Journal Reflections

Where have you underestimated yourself?
What divine abilities or gifts do you
sense God strengthening?
What would life look like if you walked
confidently in your calling?

Journaling Space

____

____

____

____

____

____

____

____

____

I Rise Declaration

I walk in God-given confidence.
Rising is my assignment, wisdom is my gift,
and resting in God is my inheritance.

Prayer

Lord, be my confidence. Strengthen my steps and
steady my heart. Let every place where I have shrunk
rise again in Your power. Amen.

I Rise Practice

Write down three strengths God has developed in you.
Speak them aloud until confidence awakens.

____

____

____

____

____

____

I Rise Affirmation

I rise confident, capable, and crowned
with God's strength.

Day 7: The Gratitude

I Rise Guarded in Mind

"In everything give thanks; for this is the will of God in Christ Jesus for you" (1 Thessalonians 5:18 NKJV).

Devotional Reading

Gratitude is the doorway to joy. It is the spiritual lens that helps you see God's fingerprints in the ordinary and the extraordinary.

Gratitude does not always change your circumstances, but it always changes you. It softens the heart, brightens the mind, and opens the spirit.

Gratitude invites God's presence into the places that felt heavy. It is a gentle reminder that even here, especially here, God is near.

Today, gratitude rises like incense in your life.

Meditation Prompt

What am I grateful for in this moment?

Journal Reflections

What blessings have I overlooked?
What has God done for me recently that
I need to acknowledge?
How does gratitude shift my emotional
or spiritual posture?

Journaling Space

I Rise Declaration

I choose gratitude in all things. Rising is my assignment,
wisdom is my gift, and resting in God is my inheritance.

Prayer

Lord, awaken gratitude in me. Help me see Your hand
at work in every corner of my life. Amen.

I Rise Practice

Write a gratitude list of seven things;
one for each day of this week's journey.

____

____

____

____

____

____

____

____

____

I Rise Affirmation

**I rise grateful, grounded, and growing
in God's goodness.**

Section II

I Heal

DAY 8: THE ALIGNMENT

I Heal Anchored in His Love

"In all your ways acknowledge Him, and He shall direct your paths" (Proverbs 3:6 NKJV).

Devotional Reading

Alignment is the holy meeting place between your will and God's way. It is where the Spirit fine-tunes your steps and straightens what life has bent.

Alignment does not mean perfection. It means positioning. It is choosing to walk in rhythm with Heaven, even when the path is unfamiliar.

When your heart aligns with God, confusion loses power, clarity returns, and purpose flows with ease.

Today is a day of divine alignment. Heaven is straightening your path.

Meditation Prompt

Where is God aligning my steps today?

Journal Reflections

What areas of my life feel out of alignment?
Where do I sense God calling me into adjustment?
What shifts must I make to walk more
closely with Him?

Journaling Space

____

____

____

____

____

____

____

____

I Rise Declaration

I align my heart, mind, and steps with God.
Rising is my assignment, wisdom is my gift,
and resting in God is my inheritance.

Prayer

Lord, bring my life into alignment with Your will.
Direct my steps and keep my path straight. Amen.

I Rise Practice

Identify one area needing alignment. Write the
adjustment and commit to one aligned action today.

I Rise Affirmation

**I rise aligned, guided, and moving
in God's direction.**

DAY 9: THE COURAGE

I Heal with Vulnerability and Bravery

"Be strong and courageous. Do not be afraid; do not be discouraged, for the Lord your God will be with you wherever you go" (Joshua 1:9 NIV).

Devotional Reading

Courage is the quiet power that rises when trust grows deeper than fear. It is not the absence of trembling, but the presence of God in the trembling.

Courage meets you where your faith and your vulnerability intersect. It reminds you that you are never walking alone. God goes before you, stands beside you, and strengthens you.

Some doors only open to the courageous. Some breakthroughs only manifest when you step forward.

If God is calling you toward it, He has already placed courage within you to reach it.

Meditation Prompt

Where is God calling me to exercise courage today?

Journal Reflections

What fear has been holding me back?
What courageous step am I being invited to take?
How has God shown Himself strong
for me in the past?

Journaling Space

____

____

____

____

____

____

____

I Rise Declaration

I choose courage over fear. Rising is my assignment, wisdom is my gift, and resting in God is my inheritance.

Prayer

Lord, strengthen my heart. Let courage rise in me like fire. Lead me with boldness and let not fear hinder what You have ordained. Amen.

I Rise Practice

Take one courageous step today, small or large, toward something God has placed in your spirit.
What have you feared that God has spoken?
Are you now ready to step out on it?

____

____

____

____

____

____

____

____

____

I Rise Affirmation

**I rise courageous, bold, and upheld
by God's strength.**

DAY 10: THE TRUST

I Heal in Ordered Steps

*"Those who trust in the LORD are like Mount Zion,
which cannot be shaken but endures forever"*
(Psalm 125:1 NIV).

Devotional Reading

Trust is the quiet strength that anchors the soul. It is the sacred confidence that God is working even when you cannot see movement.

Trust is not passive. It is active surrender. It is choosing to believe God's character over your circumstances. It is resting in the truth that God is incapable of failing you.

When trust deepens, fear loses its language. Anxiety loses its grip. Doubt loses its throne.

Today, God invites you into a deeper trust; one that steadies you like a mountain.

Meditation Prompt

Where is God asking me to deepen my trust?

Journal Reflections

What areas of my life feel unsteady?
How has God proven trustworthy in my past?
What would my life look like if I trusted Him completely in this area?

Journaling Space

____

____

____

____

____

____

____

I Rise Declaration

I trust God fully and without hesitation.
Rising is my assignment, wisdom is my gift,
and resting in God is my inheritance.

Prayer

Lord, teach me to trust You more deeply. Anchor my heart in Your faithfulness. Let my life reflect unshakable trust in who You are. Amen.

I Rise Practice

Identify one area you've been worrying about. Release it into God's hands today.

____

____

____

____

____

____

____

____

I Rise Affirmation

I rise steady, secure, and anchored in God's unfailing trustworthiness.

DAY 11: THE HOPE

I Heal Trusting in the Waiting

"May the God of hope fill you with all joy and peace as you trust in Him, so that you may overflow with hope by the power of the Holy Spirit" (Romans 15:13 NIV).

Devotional Reading

Hope is the holy whisper that tells your soul, "It is not over." It is the gentle assurance that God is still writing, still weaving, still redeeming.

Hope does not deny reality. It declares a greater reality. It is the spiritual courage to believe in God's future while standing in your present.

Hope is a lifeline. A lantern. A breath of light.

When hope rises, heaviness breaks and expectation awakens.

Today, hope is returning to you in waves.

Meditation Prompt

What hope is God restoring in me today?

Journal Reflections

Where have I felt hopeless or weary?
What promise from God am I being reminded of today?
What would it feel like to overflow with hope again?

Journaling Space

____

____

____

____

____

____

____

____

I Rise Declaration

I overflow with hope by the power of the Holy Spirit.
Rising is my assignment, wisdom is my gift, and resting
in God is my inheritance.

Prayer

God of hope, breathe life into every place that has
grown dim. Let Your joy and peace fill me until hope
overflows. Amen.

I Rise Practice

Write down one promise God has made you. Meditate
on it and speak hope into it today.

____

____

____

____

____

____

____

____

____

I Rise Affirmation

I rise filled with hope, joy, and divine expectation.

Day 12: The Peace

I Heal Through the Word

"You will keep him in perfect peace whose mind is stayed on You, because he trusts in You"
(Isaiah 26:3 NKJV).

Devotional Reading

Peace is not the absence of storms. It is the presence of God within them. It is the holy calm that settles your spirit even when life is unsettled.

Peace is not passive; it is powerful. It guards, stabilizes, soothes, and strengthens. It quiets the noise of fear and amplifies the voice of God.

Perfect peace is the portion of those who fix their minds on Him.

Today, peace is not visiting you. Peace is clothing you.

Meditation Prompt

Where do I need God's perfect peace today?

Journal Reflections

What thoughts have been disturbing my peace?
What truth from God's Word can I anchor my mind to?
How does peace shift my emotional
or spiritual posture?

Journaling Space

____

____

____

____

____

____

____

I Rise Declaration

God's perfect peace keeps my heart and mind.
Rising is my assignment, wisdom is my gift,
and resting in God is my inheritance.

Prayer

Lord, still my mind and hold my heart in Your perfect peace. Let Your presence quiet every storm within me. Amen.

I Rise Practice

Take three slow breaths, repeating silently: "God is here…I am at peace." Write three things that you are surrendering to maintain your peace.

____

____

____

____

____

____

____

____

I Rise Affirmation

I rise wrapped in perfect peace and sustained by God's presence.

Day 13: The Clarity

I Heal Remembering God's Goodness

"The unfolding of Your words gives light; it gives understanding to the simple" (Psalm 119:130 NIV).

Devotional Reading

Clarity is the light that breaks through spiritual fog. It is the moment when God's wisdom cuts through confusion and brings understanding where uncertainty once lived.

Clarity is a gift in the form of an unfolding or a holy illumination. It does not always answer every question, but it reveals the next faithful step. When clarity comes, unrest settles, discernment sharpens, and peace returns.

Today, God is releasing clarity into places where you have longed for understanding.

Meditation Prompt

Where do I need God-given clarity today?

Journal Reflections

What areas have felt confusing or overwhelming?
What insight or direction do I sense
God revealing now?
How does clarity shift my emotional
or spiritual posture?

Journaling Space

____

____

____

____

____

____

____

I Rise Declaration

I walk in divine clarity and holy understanding.
Rising is my assignment, wisdom is my gift,
and resting in God is my inheritance.

Prayer

Lord, unfold Your wisdom before me. Let Your light give understanding where I need it most. Guide my steps with holy clarity. Amen.

I Rise Practice

Write the one decision or next step you need clarity on. Sit quietly for two minutes and ask God to illuminate what is next. Record any insight, scripture, or impression that rises in your spirit.

____

____

____

____

____

____

____

____

____

I Rise Affirmation

**I rise illuminated, guided, and clear
in God's wisdom.**

DAY 14: THE JOY

I Heal in Fresh Strength

"The joy of the LORD is your strength"
(Nehemiah 8:10 NKJV).

Devotional Reading

Joy is not an emotion. Joy is a strength. It is the spiritual force that lifts you when life tries to pull you low. Joy is the echo of Heaven inside the human heart.

Joy is not dependent on circumstances. Joy flows from communion with God. Joy rises when gratitude opens the door. Joy settles when peace makes room. Joy sustains you when the journey stretches your faith.

Today, God is restoring joy where heaviness once lived. Joy is returning to your mind, your countenance, your atmosphere, and your rising.

This is not temporary joy. This is strengthening joy, sustaining joy, joy that carries you into your next season.

Meditation Prompt

Where is God restoring joy in my life today?

Journal Reflections

What moments recently brought me joy, even if small?
What has tried to steal my joy in this season?
Where do I sense God renewing joy within me?

Journaling Space

____

____

____

____

____

____

____

I Rise Declaration

I choose joy and joy strengthens me.
Rising is my assignment, wisdom is my gift,
and resting in God is my inheritance.

Prayer

Lord, restore the joy of my salvation. Let Your joy rise
in me until it overflows. Strengthen my heart with
divine gladness and let joy carry me forward
in Your purpose. Amen.

I Rise Practice

Do one small thing today that brings you joy.
Take a walk. Sing a song. Have a moment of praise.
Take a breath of gratitude. Let joy move through you.
Write your song/poem of praise to God.

I Rise Affirmation

**I rise strengthened, renewed, and lifted
by the joy of the Lord.**

Section III

I Lead

DAY 15: THE FAVOR

I Lead with a Purified Heart

"For You, O LORD, will bless the righteous; with favor
You will surround him as with a shield"
(Psalm 5:12 NKJV).

Devotional Reading

Favor is the divine advantage God places on your life. It is the unseen endorsement of Heaven. God's "yes" resting on your steps and your assignments.

Favor is not random; favor is relational. It flows from intimacy, obedience, alignment, and surrender.

Favor opens doors no man can close. Favor positions you where preparation meets opportunity. Favor surrounds you like a shield. It protects you, covers you, and advances you.

Today, God is renewing, restoring, and releasing fresh favor over your life. Walk in it. Expect it. Carry it with humility and confidence. You are favored by God.

Meditation Prompt

Where do I sense the favor of God
moving in my life right now?

Journal Reflections

Where have I seen God's favor in previous seasons?
What would it look like to walk boldly in
the favor I already have?
How can I steward God's favor with
integrity and humility?

Journaling Space

I Rise Declaration

God's favor surrounds me like a shield.
Rising is my assignment, wisdom is my gift,
and resting in God is my inheritance.

Prayer

Lord, thank You for Your divine favor. Surround me
with Your blessing, guide me with Your wisdom, and
position me for every assignment You have ordained.
Let my life reflect Your goodness. Amen.

I Rise Practice

Speak favor over one area of your life today.
Your health, your work, your ministry,
your relationships, or your purpose.
Identify what favor means to you.

____

____

____

____

I Rise Affirmation

**I rise favored, covered, and positioned
by God's goodness.**

DAY 16: THE STRENGTH

I Lead Reclaiming Joy

*"But those who wait on the LORD shall renew their
strength; they shall mount up with wings like eagles…"*
(Isaiah 40:31 NKJV).

Devotional Reading

Strength is more than endurance. It is the divine
infusion of power that comes from waiting in
God's presence.

Waiting is not idleness; waiting is spiritual exchange.
It is where your weakness is traded for God's strength,
your fatigue for His renewal, your uncertainty for His
confidence.

Eagles do not strive to soar; they ascend because the
wind carries them. So, it is when God renews your
strength, you rise without straining.

Today, God is strengthening you in the deep places of your spirit, mind, emotions, and body. You will run again. You will soar again. You will not faint.

Meditation Prompt

Where do I need God to renew my strength today?

Journal Reflections

What has been draining my strength recently?
Where do I feel God lifting or renewing me?
How does God strengthen me differently than
people or circumstances do?

Journaling Space

____

____

____

____

____

____

I Rise Declaration

God renews my strength daily. Rising is my assignment, wisdom is my gift, and resting in God is my inheritance.

Prayer

Lord, renew my strength. Lift me where I am weary.
Empower me where I feel weak. Let me soar on the
wind of Your Spirit and walk with resilience,
endurance, and grace. Amen.

I Rise Practice

Take a 60-second pause today.
Breathe deeply and invite God to refill your strength.
What are you asking God to do for you today?

____

____

____

____

____

____

____

____

____

I Rise Affirmation

**I rise renewed, strengthened, and upheld
by the power of God.**

DAY 17: THE DISCERNMENT

I Lead Gentle Within Myself

"Your ears shall hear a word behind you, saying, 'This is the way, walk in it,' whenever you turn…"
(Isaiah 30:21 NKJV).

Devotional Reading

Discernment is the spiritual ability to sense God's voice, God's direction, and God's timing. It is more than intuition. It is divine intelligence.

Discernment is the compass of the Spirit. It reveals what is of God and what is not. It exposes what is distraction and what is destiny. It helps you recognize the difference between a good opportunity and a God opportunity.

Discernment sharpens through closeness with God. The more you commune with Him, the more clearly you perceive His leading.

Today, God is heightening your discernment: your hearing, your sensing, your knowing. You will hear the whisper. You will know the way. And you will not miss God.

Meditation Prompt

Where is God sharpening my discernment today?

Journal Reflections

What decisions or relationships require
discernment right now?
Where do I feel the Spirit guiding me?
What distractions or voices do I need to silence?

Journaling Space

____

____

____

____

____

____

____

I Rise Declaration

I walk in divine discernment. Rising is my assignment, wisdom is my gift, and resting in God is my inheritance.

Prayer

Holy Spirit, sharpen my hearing. Illuminate my path. Whisper "This is the way" and steady my feet in the direction of Your will. Remove confusion, silence false voices, and lead me into divine alignment. Amen.

I Rise Practice

Spend five minutes listening in silence. No asking or analyzing. Only listening for the whisper of God. What did God whisper in your spirit?

____

____

____

____

____

____

I Rise Affirmation

**I rise discerning, Spirit-led, and directed
by God's voice.**

Day 18: The Release

I Lead Boldly

"Cast your burden on the LORD, and He shall sustain you…" (Psalm 55:22 NKJV).

Devotional Reading

Release is the doorway to freedom. It is the sacred act of placing what weighs you down into the hands of the God who sustains you.

Release is not weakness. Release is wisdom. It is choosing not to carry what God never designed for you to hold.

Burdened hearts cannot rise. Tightened fists cannot receive. But when you truly release, something in your soul exhales.

Today, Heaven invites you to let go: let go of the old emotion, the old wound, the old disappointment, the old fear.

God cannot fill what you refuse to release. But the moment you release, God sustains you, completely, lovingly, and faithfully.

Meditation Prompt

What burden have I been carrying that
God is asking me to release?

Journal Reflections

What emotional weight have I been holding onto?
What fear, memory, or disappointment
is ready to be released?
How does release create space in my soul for renewal?

Journaling Space

____

____

____

____

____

____

____

I Rise Declaration

I release what no longer serves my rising.
Rising is my assignment, wisdom is my gift,
and resting in God is my inheritance.

Prayer

Lord, I release every burden into Your hands. Lift the
weight from my spirit. Sustain me with Your strength
and surround me with Your peace. Help me to let go
fully so I may rise freely. Amen.

I Rise Practice

Write down one burden and speak aloud: "God, I
release this into Your hands." Tear up the paper as a
prophetic act of freedom.

____

____

____

____

____

____

I Rise Affirmation

I rise free, unburdened, and sustained by God.

DAY 19: THE HEALING

I Lead Fruitfully in Every Season

"He heals the brokenhearted and binds up their wounds"
(Psalm 147:3 NKJV).

Devotional Reading

Healing is a divine process, not a moment. It unfolds gently, like morning light easing into a dark room.

Healing does not always begin with relief; sometimes it begins with honesty by acknowledging what hurt, what broke, and what was lost.

But God does not leave wounds exposed. He binds, restores and heals from the inside out.

Today, God is tending to your heart. He is applying oil to old wounds and stitching together places that felt torn. You are being made whole.

Meditation Prompt

What part of my heart needs God's
healing touch today?

Journal Reflections

What past wound still aches in my
memory or emotions?
How do I sense God bringing healing
into that area now?
What would wholeness look like for me?

Journaling Space

____

____

____

____

____

____

____

I Rise Declaration

I am healing and whole in God.
Rising is my assignment, wisdom is my gift,
and resting in God is my inheritance.

Prayer

Great Healer, touch every broken place in me. Bind what is wounded. Restore what has been damaged. Heal what has been hidden. Make me whole by Your power and Your love. Amen.

I Rise Practice

Write a forgiveness letter to yourself today. Let compassion speak. Let release begin. Let healing flow.

____

____

____

____

____

____

____

____

I Rise Affirmation

I rise healing, whole, and restored by God's grace.

Day 20: The Vision

I Lead Aligned with Purpose

"Write the vision and make it plain…though it tarries, wait for it; because it will surely come"
(Habakkuk 2:2-3 NKJV).

Devotional Reading

Vision is the language of destiny. It is how God whispers your future into your present.

Vision is more than imagination. It is revelation. It is Heaven showing you what is possible through God's power, not your limitations.

Vision clarifies purpose. Vision fuels perseverance. Vision pulls you forward when circumstances try to hold you back.

Every God-given vision has an appointed time. Delay does not mean denial. Waiting does not mean wasting.

Today, God is sharpening your vision, your spiritual sight, your purpose sight, your prophetic sight. Write what you see. Declare what you hear. Hold steady because the vision will come.

Meditation Prompt

What vision is God reviving, expanding,
or birthing in me now?

Journal Reflections

What has God shown me about
my purpose or future?
What vision have I delayed writing,
pursuing, or believing?
What clarity is God giving me right now?

Journaling Space

____

____

____

____

____

____

____

I Rise Declaration

I receive God's vision for my life.
Rising is my assignment, wisdom is my gift,
and resting in God is my inheritance.

Prayer

Lord, breathe on my vision. Sharpen my sight.
Strengthen my faith. Give me boldness to write, pursue,
and protect what You have revealed. Let Your
appointed time manifest in my life. Amen.

I Rise Practice

Write one vision God has placed in your spirit.
Draw a simple outline of what it could become.
This is your seed.

____

____

____

____

____

____

I Rise Affirmation

**I rise visionary, focused, and aligned with
God's appointed time.**

DAY 21: THE BECOMING

I Lead from Glory to Glory

"Beloved, now we are children of God; and it has not yet been revealed what we shall be…" (1 John 3:2 NKJV).

Devotional Reading

Rising is not a moment. Rising is a journey, a transformation, a holy unfolding.

You have walked through beginnings, unveilings, awakenings, stillness, surrender, strength, clarity, trust, healing, vision…and now you stand at the threshold of rising.

Rising means stepping into the version of you God always saw, even when you could not see it. It means embracing your identity, your purpose, your calling, your fullness.

Rising is not trying. It is aligning and resting in who God says you are.

You are not who you were on Day 1. You are not who you were yesterday. You are rising, daily, deeply, beautifully. And this is only the beginning.

Meditation Prompt

What part of me has blossomed the
most during these 21 days?

Journal Reflections

What shifts have taken place within me?
What truths do I now embrace?
What next step is God calling me to take
in my rising journey?

Journaling Space

____

____

____

____

____

____

____

I Rise Declaration

I am rising into everything God designed me to be.
Rising is my assignment, wisdom is my gift,
and resting in God is my inheritance.

Prayer

Lord, thank You for every moment of rising. For every
whisper, every revelation, every shift, every healing,
every awakening. I surrender fully to who You are
shaping me to be. Let my life reflect Your glory and my
journey reveal Your faithfulness. Amen.

I Rise Practice

Write a letter to your future self, to the you who is fully
walking in purpose, grace, and identity. Seal it.
Return to it in one year.

____

____

____

____

____

____

____

I Rise Affirmation

I rise beautifully, boldly, completely God's.

As the Journey Continues

You have walked through twenty-one days of reflection, prayer, and rising awareness. Each day invited you to pause, listen, release, and receive. Some moments may have stirred deep healing. Others may have awakened new clarity about the path ahead.

Yet the journey of rising does not end with the final page of this devotional. It continues in the choices you make each day; in the courage to walk forward, the faith to trust God's guidance, and the wisdom to lead with compassion and integrity.

The prayers you have spoken over these twenty-one days are seeds planted in your spirit. In the days ahead, those seeds will continue to grow as you walk faithfully in the purpose God has placed within you.

Before you move forward, receive this blessing as a reminder that you do not walk alone. The same grace that carried you through these days will continue to guide your steps.

CLOSING REFLECTION:
THE WOMAN WHO RISES

You began this journey with a whisper. Perhaps it was a quiet stirring in your spirit, a gentle awareness that something within you was ready to change. Maybe you opened this devotional seeking clarity, healing, strength, or direction. Whatever brought you here, you did not arrive by accident.

Over the past twenty-one days, you have walked through moments of reflection, courage, stillness, surrender, gratitude, discernment, healing, and vision. You have faced your thoughts honestly. You have listened for the voice of God. You have taken steps, small and brave, toward becoming the woman God designed you to be. And now you stand here. Not at the end of the journey, but at the beginning of a new chapter.

The woman who rises is not defined by perfection. She is defined by persistence. She does not pretend life is

easy, nor does she allow difficulty to silence her faith. She knows that growth is a process and that transformation unfolds day by day.

The woman who rises remembers that God is faithful in every season. She rises when she feels strong. She rises when she feels uncertain. She rises when healing is still unfolding. She rises because she trusts the One who called her forward.

Your rising will not always look dramatic. Often it will appear in quiet decisions such as choosing peace when anxiety tries to return, choosing truth when doubt whispers lies, choosing courage when fear suggests retreat, or choosing compassion for yourself as you continue to grow. Every time you choose alignment with God's wisdom, you rise again.

Carry what you have learned into the days ahead. Continue listening for God's guidance. Continue practicing gratitude, courage, and surrender. Continue strengthening the habits that nurture your spirit.

You are not the same woman who began on Day One. You are wiser. You are stronger. You are more aware of the presence of God within your life.

The journey of rising continues every day you choose faith over fear and purpose over hesitation. Rise again tomorrow. Rise again next week. Rise again whenever life invites you to grow.

And remember: Rising is my assignment, wisdom is my gift, and resting in God is my inheritance.

Closing Prayer

Gracious God, thank You for the journey of these twenty-one days. Thank You for every moment of reflection, every insight, every gentle correction, and every quiet reminder that Your presence has never left me.

You have walked with me through awakening and surrender, through healing and clarity, through courage and vision. You have reminded me that my life is not defined by my past but by the purpose You continue to unfold before me. Help me carry these lessons forward.

When fear tries to return, remind me that Your strength surrounds me. When doubt whispers, remind me of the truth of Your Word. When the path ahead feels uncertain, remind me that You are guiding every step. Teach me to rise daily with humility, wisdom, and courage.

Let this not be the end of a journey, but the establishment of a new way of living. What You have begun in me, O God, is not temporary. It is transformational. Seal these truths within my spirit so they are not easily shaken by circumstance or emotion. I choose to walk forward with intention, not drifting, not returning, but advancing in the identity You have restored within me.

I declare that I will not abandon what I have learned in moments of pressure. I will stand on it. I will live it. I will lead from it. Let my life become evidence of Your grace, Your power, and Your faithfulness. Use me as a vessel of clarity for others who are still searching, still healing, still rising. And as I move into what is next, I do so with full confidence that the same God who carried me through these days will sustain me in every season ahead.

Your Word declares in Philippians 1:6 (NKJV), *"Being confident of this very thing, that He who has begun a good work in you will complete it until the day of Jesus Christ."*

Let my life reflect Your goodness. Let my words bring encouragement. Let my actions create peace wherever You send me. Strengthen me to lead with compassion, to serve with integrity, and to walk with the quiet confidence that comes from knowing I am held in Your care.

As this devotional journey concludes, let the deeper journey of transformation continue. May I rise with grace. May I rise with purpose. May I rise with faith. And may everything I do bring honor to You. Amen.

Pastoral Blessing / Legacy Message

To my family, both natural and spiritual, this book carries your imprint. Your love has steadied me. Your prayers have covered me. Your faith has strengthened my hands.

To my two sisters, Mary and Linda, I pray nightly for your joy, peace, love and prosperity. I remember with gratitude every act of kindness and I release everything in between. May God surround you with favor and fill your days with quiet strength.

To my precious and kindhearted nephew, Key, you are an answered prayer in motion. I rejoice over the hope, healing, and wholeness God continues to reveal in you. You are beautiful inside and out. You inspire me daily to believe for more and to expect God for greater.

To my Tabernacle of Alpha & Omega Church family, who have trusted my voice, received my counsel, and allowed me to teach, shepherd, and pour: thank you.

To my sons and daughters in the Gospel, you are not accidental. You are entrusted. Rise with discipline. Lead with humility. Guard what has been placed in your hands.

May your influence be rooted in integrity, and your authority be anchored in surrender. Go further than I have gone. Build stronger than I have built. Carry wisdom responsibly into every space you enter. You are covered, called, and capable. Walk accordingly.

May these 21 days draw you into deeper becoming. May you lay hold of your inheritance in Christ. May you rise as joint-heirs, warriors of wisdom, and stewards of glory.

And to every reader who opens these pages with hope in your heart: May the oil of these words bring healing, awakening, rest, and renewal. May they speak life into your now, strength into your becoming, and courage into your future.

This devotional is my offering, my love, my prayer, and my legacy.

Dr. Carolyn Coleman
The Lady of Wisdom

A Blessing for the Woman Who Rises

May the God of wisdom guide your steps as you continue the journey of rising.

May your heart remain anchored in truth and your mind filled with clarity and peace.

May courage meet you in moments of uncertainty, and may grace strengthen you when the path feels difficult.

May healing continue in the quiet places of your soul. May every wound find restoration and every burden find release.

May your voice grow stronger with each passing season, and may the wisdom within you illuminate the lives of others.

May your faith remain steady when circumstances change.

May your spirit be refreshed when the journey requires patience.

May you walk confidently in the purpose God has placed within you, trusting that the One who began a good work in you will faithfully bring it to completion.

May your life reflect light in places that need hope, peace in moments that require calm, and compassion wherever your presence is felt.

And when the days ahead invite you to rise again, may you remember the truth that has carried you this far:

You are called.
You are strengthened.
You are guided.

Rise with courage.
Rise with wisdom.
Rise with grace.

And may the presence of God walk with you in every step of the journey ahead.

Amen.

The 21-Day Rising Tracker

Mark your progress as you move through the devotional journey.

Completed	Day	Title
☐	Day 1	The Beginning
☐	Day 2	The Unveiling
☐	Day 3	The Awakening
☐	Day 4	The Stillness
☐	Day 5	The Surrender
☐	Day 6	The Confidence
☐	Day 7	The Gratitude
☐	Day 8	The Alignment
☐	Day 9	The Courage
☐	Day 10	The Trust
☐	Day 11	The Hope
☐	Day 12	The Peace
☐	Day 13	The Clarity
☐	Day 14	The Joy
☐	Day 15	The Favor
☐	Day 16	The Strength
☐	Day 17	The Discernment
☐	Day 18	The Release
☐	Day 19	The Healing
☐	Day 20	The Vision
☐	Day 21	The Becoming

Reflection Space

Start Date: _______________________________

Completion Date: _______________________________

What changed in me during these 21 days?

____

____

____

____

____

____

____

____

____

____

____

____

____

____

Final Rising Commitment

My next step in this season of rising:

____

____

____

____

____

____

____

____

____

____

____

____

____

____

APPENDICES

APPENDIX A:
VIBRATIONS OF HEALING

Healing is rarely loud. It often begins as a quiet shift, a softening of the heart, a loosening of tension in the soul, a gentle breath where pain once lived. Healing moves in subtle waves, like vibrations traveling through the deepest places of the spirit.

Sometimes healing comes through prayer. Sometimes through tears. Sometimes through truth spoken at the right moment. And sometimes healing begins simply because you finally gave yourself permission to stop carrying what God never asked you to hold.

Healing is not weakness. Healing is restoration.

Scripture reminds us:

"He heals the brokenhearted and binds up their wounds"
(Psalm 147:3).

God does not ignore wounds. He tends to them. He sits with us in our sorrow, speaks peace into our confusion, and gently restores what life tried to fracture.

Healing may take time. It may unfold layer by layer. But every step toward wholeness is sacred.

As you continue your rising journey, remember that healing is not something you force. Healing is something you allow. Allow truth to replace shame. Allow grace to replace self-judgment. Allow God's presence to fill the spaces where pain once lived.

Your healing matters. Your wholeness matters. And every vibration of healing within you is evidence that God is still restoring your life.

Healing Reflection Questions

- What part of my heart still needs gentle attention?
- Where do I sense God bringing restoration into my life?
- What truth do I need to accept in order to move toward healing?

Write freely. Let honesty lead you.

____

____

____

____

____

____

____

____

____

____

____

A Prayer for Healing

Father, You see every hidden wound and every silent burden. Nothing in my life is invisible to You.

Where my heart has been broken, bring restoration. Where my mind has been troubled, bring peace. Where my spirit has grown weary, breathe renewal.

Teach me to release what I cannot change and to trust the healing You are working within me.

Restore my joy. Strengthen my spirit. Renew my hope. I receive Your healing with humility and gratitude. Amen.

Healing Affirmation

I am healing. God is restoring every place within me that once felt broken. My life is moving toward wholeness, peace, and renewal.

Appendix B:
Rising for Teens

A Rising Guide for Ages 13–18

Rising in adolescence is real formation. Many teens are carrying pressure that looks normal on the outside but feels heavy on the inside. It could be a result of mental strain, online influence, bullying, identity questions, academic overload, and support gaps.

This section is not here to shame you. It is here to strengthen you. You don't have to have perfect words to ask for help. You just have to rise toward safety.

The Teen Rising Pledge

I rise with truth.
I rise with wisdom. I rise with courage.
I will not carry pain in silence.

I will not hide in darkness.
I will speak to someone safe.
I will choose life.

Support Gaps and
"I Rise" Declarations for Teens

1. When Your Mind Feels Heavy

I Rise with breath and courage. I am not broken because I feel deeply. My thoughts do not frighten me, and my emotions do not control me. I give myself permission to pause, breathe, and ask for help. I am learning. I am safe while I grow.

2. When the Screen Challenges Your Worth

I Rise above comparison. My value is not measured by likes, views, or approval. I trust my voice more than the noise around me. I choose clarity. I choose kindness toward myself.

3. When Bullying or Cyberbullying Hurts

I Rise protected and supported. I refuse to carry words that were not spoken in love. What others project is not my identity. I choose connection over silence. I am worthy of respect and protection.

4. When School Feels Like Too Much

I Rise through growth, not perfection. I am more than my grades. Mistakes do not cancel my future. They develop my strength. Progress is happening even when it feels slow.

5. When the Mirror Feels Unkind

I Rise with gentleness. My body is my home, not my enemy. I speak to myself with respect. I am not rushed. I am not ashamed. I am enough in this moment.

6. When Rest Feels Out of Reach

I Rise rested and steady. Slowing down restores me. Peace is allowed to find me. Sleep is not weakness. Rest is wisdom.

7. When You Feel Pressured to "Go Along"

I Rise with boundaries. I can say no without guilt. My choices matter. I protect my well-being because my future is valuable.

8. When Fitting In Feels Necessary

I Rise authentic. I will not disappear to belong. The right people will recognize me as I am. I choose integrity over approval.

9. When You Want Independence but Feel Unsure

I Rise with grace for the process. I don't have to have all the answers now. This season is for learning, not perfection. Clarity will come.

10. When You Feel Unseen

I Rise seen and worthy. My feelings are valid even when they're hard to explain. I deserve support. I am not invisible. I matter.

The "3 Safe People" Rule

Choose three safe people you can talk to when life feels heavy:

1. ____

2. ____

3. ____

If you or a teen you love is in immediate danger or considering self-harm, contact local emergency services right away. If you are in the U.S., you can call or text **988** for the Suicide & Crisis Lifeline.

APPENDIX C:
RISING PARENTING ACTIVATION GUIDE

For Parents, Pastors, Educators, and Youth Leaders

You are not raising "kids." You are shaping **carriers** of identity, future, faith, and purpose. And in this generation, silence is not neutral. **Silence is risk.** So, we lead with wisdom, tenderness, and clear authority.

The Parent Leader Mandate

- I will not minimize distress.
- I will not shame emotion.
- I will not ignore warning signs.

- I will cover my child with presence, truth, structure, and help.

Weekly Family Conversation Questions (15 minutes)

1. What pressure are you feeling that you haven't said out loud?
2. Where do you feel unseen?
3. What does "rising" look like for you this week?
4. Who do you trust enough to talk to when you feel overwhelmed?
5. What would support look like, specifically, this week?

Warning Sign Awareness Checklist

Be alert to:

- Withdrawal from normal activity
- Sudden changes in sleep or appetite
- Language of hopelessness or worthlessness
- Social isolation
- Increased secrecy
- Emotional volatility or rage
- Giving away possessions or "goodbye" messages

This doesn't create fear. It creates coverage.

The "3-Check" Protocol
(Simple. Weekly. Effective.)

1. **Check the Heart:** "How are you really doing inside?"
2. **Check the Environment:** "Who are you around online and offline?"
3. **Check the Support:** "Who can you talk to besides me?"

What to Say (Scripts that build safety)

- "I'm not here to punish you. I'm here to protect you."
- "You can tell me the hard part. I can handle it."
- "We're going to get help. We're doing this together."
- "Your life matters too much for silence."

What **NOT** to Say
(Because it shuts them down)

- "You're being dramatic."
- "Other people have it worse."
- "Just pray and get over it."
- "Why would you think like that?"

Prayer is power, **but presence is proof**.

When You Need More Support

If danger is immediate, call emergency services. If you're in the U.S., call/text **988**.

If you're unsure, don't wait: consult a licensed counselor, pediatrician, school counselor, or pastor who understands mental health care.

Appendix D:
The I Rise and Heal Workshop Kit

Workshop Formats

Choose one:

- 60 minutes (single session)
- 90 minutes (deep activation)
- 4-week series (best for churches)

Workshop Title Options

- I Rise: A Night of Healing and Strength
- I Rise: Identity, Peace, and Purpose
- I Rise: Family Leadership Activation Night

90-Minute Workshop Flow (Pro-ready)

1) Welcome and Covering (10 min)

Open with:

"This is not performance. This is formation."

Group declaration: **"This is my new now and I rise."**

2) Teaching Module (20 min)

Pick ONE:
- Rising in Identity (2 Timothy 1:7)
- Rising in Peace (Isaiah 26:3)
- Rising in Vision (Habakkuk 2:2–3)

Teaching structure (3 movements):
1. What's attacking in this season
2. What God says (scripture)
3. What rising looks like (action)

3) Guided Reflection and Writing (15 min)

Prompts:
- Where am I shrinking?
- What am I carrying that isn't mine?
- What is my one rising decision this week?

4) Activation (15 min)

Participants choose ONE:
- An "I Rise" affirmation for the week
- A "Release list" (3 burdens)
- A "Support map" (3 safe people)

5) **Prayer and Ministry Moment (20 min)**

Prayer for healing, clarity, courage, and family protection.
Optional: altar call for those needing support.

6) **Close and Call to Action (10 min)**

Charge:
"You don't need permission to rise. You need ownership."
Invite group to continue the 21-day reading plan together.

Appendix E:
AI Faith & Authority

Wisdom, Discernment, and
the Future of Leadership

Artificial intelligence is changing how the world communicates, learns, and leads. From education and healthcare to ministry and creative work, technology now shapes daily life in ways previous generations could not imagine.

Yet while technology evolves, one truth remains unchanged: **wisdom must lead innovation**. Technology without wisdom becomes noise. Technology without discernment becomes influence without direction. But when wisdom leads, technology becomes a tool for service, learning, and global connection.

Faith in a Digital Age

Scripture reminds us:

"Wisdom is the principal thing; therefore get wisdom"
(Proverbs 4:7).

Rising with Wisdom

The future will belong to leaders who combine **faith, wisdom, and thoughtful innovation**. Let technology serve your calling. Let wisdom guide your influence. Let discernment protect your voice.

As the world evolves, remain anchored in truth. **And continue rising.**

Biblical Foundations for Wisdom and Discernment

Scripture reminds believers that wisdom and discernment are gifts from God. As new tools and technologies emerge, our responsibility is not to respond with fear but to seek divine wisdom in how we use them. Throughout the Bible, God consistently instructs His people to pursue knowledge, understanding, and wise stewardship of the resources entrusted to them.

Proverbs 4:7

"Wisdom is the principal thing; therefore get wisdom. And in all your getting, get understanding." (NKJV)

This verse reminds us that knowledge alone is not enough. Wisdom guides how knowledge is applied. Technology may expand our access to information, but believers must always apply spiritual wisdom in how they interpret and use what they learn.

Daniel 1:17

"As for these four young men, God gave them knowledge and skill in all literature and wisdom; and Daniel had understanding in all visions and dreams." (NKJV)

Daniel and his companions were trained in the most advanced knowledge of their time while remaining faithful to God. Their example reminds us that engaging with learning and innovation does not diminish faith when it is grounded in obedience to God.

James 1:5

"If any of you lacks wisdom, let him ask of God, who gives to all liberally and without reproach, and it will be given to him." (NKJV)

This promise reassures believers that when facing new challenges or unfamiliar tools, we are not left to navigate them alone. God invites us to ask for wisdom so that we may lead, discern, and steward responsibly.

1 Thessalonians 5:21

"Test all things; hold fast what is good." (NKJV)

Faith does not require rejecting every new development. Instead, Scripture instructs believers to examine, test, and discern carefully, keeping what aligns with truth and wisdom.

Faith Before Technology

Artificial intelligence is not a source of wisdom, revelation, or spiritual authority. It is a tool created through human innovation. Like books, printing presses, computers, and the internet before it, AI can assist in research, writing, education, and communication. However, spiritual authority remains grounded in Scripture, prayer, and the leading of the Holy Spirit.

When used responsibly, technology can support ministry, scholarship, teaching, and creative work. The key for believers is not avoidance but **wise stewardship**.

Guidelines for Faithful
Use of Artificial Intelligence

As believers engage with new technologies, wisdom and discernment remain essential. Artificial intelligence can assist learning, writing, research, and organization, but it should always be used responsibly and with spiritual awareness. The following principles help ensure that technology remains a tool rather than a source of authority.

1. Keep God as the Source of Wisdom

Scripture, prayer, and the guidance of the Holy Spirit remain the believer's foundation. Technology may assist in gathering information, but true wisdom comes from God.

"For the Lord gives wisdom; from His mouth come knowledge and understanding" (Proverbs 2:6 NKJV).

2. Use Technology as a Tool, Not a Teacher

Artificial intelligence can help organize ideas, support research, and assist creativity. However, it should never replace spiritual discernment, biblical study, or the counsel of wise leaders.

3. Practice Discernment in All Things

Not every idea or piece of information should be accepted without examination. Believers are called to test what they encounter and hold firmly to what aligns with truth.

"Beloved, do not believe every spirit, but test the spirits, whether they are of God" (1 John 4:1 NKJV).

4. Use Technology to Serve Others

Technology becomes most valuable when it helps strengthen communities, expand education, and share messages of hope, healing, and faith.

5. Lead With Integrity and Responsibility

Every tool carries responsibility. Believers must use technology ethically, truthfully, and with humility,

remembering that our words and actions represent our faith.

"And whatever you do, do it heartily, as to the Lord and not to men" (Colossians 3:23 NKJV).

A Final Reflection

Throughout history, each generation has encountered new tools that reshaped communication, learning, and ministry. The printing press expanded the reach of the Bible. Radio and television carried messages of faith across nations. The internet connected believers around the world.

Artificial intelligence represents another tool in this continuing story.

For people of faith, the question is not whether technology will exist, but **how it will be used**. When guided by wisdom, humility, and devotion to God, even modern tools can serve the purpose of spreading truth, strengthening communities, and equipping leaders for the work ahead.

A Prayer for Wisdom in a Digital World

Father, As the world continues to change, anchor my heart in wisdom. Help me use technology responsibly and with discernment. Protect my mind from distraction and my spirit from confusion.

Let every tool I use serve a greater purpose, learning, helping others, and advancing truth. Keep my heart

grounded in Your presence so that no innovation ever replaces wisdom.

Guide my steps in this digital age. Amen.

Devotional-Reader Gift

As a continuation of this experience, you are invited to receive a special gift. Use the code: BECOMING21 to receive a discounted opportunity to engage in an upcoming AI Masterclass or Consultation Session designed to help you walk boldly in clarity, wisdom, and execution.

**Scan to Continue
Your Journey**

Devotional Innovations

THE 21 RISING COMPANION QUICK REFERENCE GUIDE

A Scripture Companion for Meditation and Reflection

These scriptures anchor the journey of rising. Each passage invites you to return to the Word of God for strength, clarity, and spiritual renewal.

Day 1 – Philippians 1:6 (NKJV)

> *"Being confident of this very thing, that He who has begun a good work in you will complete it until the day of Jesus Christ."*

Day 2 – 2 Corinthians 3:18 (NIV)

> *"And we all, who with unveiled faces contemplate the Lord's glory, are being transformed into his image*

with ever-increasing glory, which comes from
the Lord, who is the Spirit."

Day 3 – Isaiah 60:1 (NIV)

"Arise, shine; for your light has come, and the glory of the
Lord rises upon you."

Day 4 – Psalm 46:10 (NKJV)

"Be still, and know that I am God."

Day 5 – Proverbs 3:5 (NIV)

"Trust in the Lord with all your heart and
lean not on your own understanding."

Day 6 – Proverbs 3:26 (NKJV)

"For the Lord will be your confidence and will
keep your foot from being caught."

Day 7 – 1 Thessalonians 5:18 (NKJV)

"In everything give thanks; for this is the will of
God in Christ Jesus for you."

Day 8 – Proverbs 3:6 (NKJV)

"In all your ways acknowledge Him,
and He shall direct your paths."

Day 9 – Joshua 1:9 (NIV)

*"Be strong and courageous. Do not be afraid;
do not be discouraged, for the Lord your
God will be with you wherever you go."*

Day 10 – Psalm 125:1 (NIV)

*"Those who trust in the Lord are like Mount Zion,
which cannot be shaken but endures forever."*

Day 11 – Romans 15:13 (NIV)

*"May the God of hope fill you with all joy and peace as
you trust in him, so that you may overflow with hope by
the power of the Holy Spirit."*

Day 12 – Isaiah 26:3 (NKJV)

*"You will keep him in perfect peace, whose mind is stayed
on You, because he trusts in You."*

Day 13 – Psalm 119:130 (NIV)

*"The unfolding of your words gives light;
it gives understanding to the simple."*

Day 14 – Nehemiah 8:10 (NKJV)

"The joy of the Lord is your strength."

Day 15 – Psalm 5:12 (NKJV)

*"For You, O Lord, will bless the righteous; with favor
You will surround him as with a shield."*

Day 16 – Isaiah 40:31 (NKJV)

*"But those who wait on the Lord shall renew their
strength; they shall mount up with wings like eagles."*

Day 17 – Isaiah 30:21 (NKJV)

*"Your ears shall hear a word behind you, saying,
'This is the way, walk in it.'"*

Day 18 – Psalm 55:22 (NKJV)

*"Cast your burden on the Lord, and
He shall sustain you."*

Day 19 – Psalm 147:3 (NKJV)

"He heals the brokenhearted and binds up their wounds."

Day 20 – Habakkuk 2:2–3 (NKJV)

*"Write the vision and make it plain…though it tarries,
wait for it; because it will surely come."*

Day 21 – 1 John 3:2 (NKJV)

*"Beloved, now we are children of God; and it has
not yet been revealed what we shall be."*

THE 21 RISING PRAYERS

A Prayer Companion for Strength, Healing, and Alignment

Sometimes the heart needs prayer before reflection. These prayers gather the petitions from each day of the devotional so that you may return to them whenever your spirit needs strengthening.

Pray them slowly. Speak them sincerely. Let each prayer guide your heart back to the presence of God.

Day 1 – Prayer for New Beginnings

Lord, thank You for beginnings. Give me courage to step forward in faith and trust the work You are doing in me. Strengthen my heart to begin again where You are calling me. Amen.

Day 2 – Prayer for Identity

Lord, reveal who You created me to be. Remove every false identity and every label that does not come from You. Let Your truth anchor my confidence and guide my life. Amen.

Day 3 – Prayer for Awakening

Lord, awaken what has been quiet within my spirit. Let Your light rise upon me and illuminate the path ahead. Renew my awareness of Your presence and purpose in my life. Amen.

Day 4 – Prayer for Stillness

Lord, quiet my thoughts and calm my heart. Help me rest in Your presence and release the noise of worry and distraction. Let Your peace restore my soul. Amen.

Day 5 – Prayer for Surrender

Lord, I release what I cannot control into Your hands. Teach me to trust Your wisdom above my understanding. Strengthen my faith to surrender fully to Your will. Amen.

Day 6 – Prayer for Confidence

Lord, be my confidence and steady my steps. Where I have doubted myself, remind me of the strength You have placed within me. Help me walk boldly in the identity You have given me. Amen.

Day 7 – Prayer for Gratitude

Lord, awaken gratitude in my heart. Help me see Your goodness in both the ordinary and the extraordinary moments of life. Let thankfulness shape my perspective and strengthen my spirit. Amen.

Day 8 – Prayer for Alignment

Lord, align my thoughts, my heart, and my steps with Your wisdom. Where I have wandered, guide me back into Your direction. Order my path and help me walk faithfully in Your purpose. Amen.

Day 9 – Prayer for Courage

Lord, strengthen my heart with courage. When fear whispers, remind me that You walk beside me. Give me boldness to step forward in faith and trust Your guidance. Amen.

Day 10 – Prayer for Trust

Lord, teach me to trust You more deeply. Anchor my heart in the assurance that You are working even when I cannot see it. Let my life reflect confidence in Your faithfulness. Amen.

Day 11 – Prayer for Hope

God of hope, breathe life into every place that has grown weary within me. Fill my heart with joy and peace as I trust in You. Let hope overflow in my spirit through the power of Your presence. Amen.

Day 12 – Prayer for Peace

Lord, quiet every storm within my mind and heart. Guard my thoughts with Your truth and surround me with Your perfect peace. Help me rest in the assurance that You are near. Amen.

Day 13 – Prayer for Clarity

Lord, unfold Your wisdom before me. Bring clarity where confusion once lived and understanding where uncertainty has lingered. Illuminate my path and guide my next steps. Amen.

Day 14 – Prayer for Joy

Lord, restore the joy of my spirit. Lift every heaviness that has settled upon my heart. Let Your joy strengthen me and renew my outlook on the days ahead. Amen.

Day 15 – Prayer for Favor

Lord, thank You for the favor that surrounds my life. Guide my steps and position me where Your purpose can unfold. Help me walk with humility, wisdom, and gratitude for Your blessing. Amen.

Day 16 – Prayer for Strength

Lord, renew my strength where I feel weary. Lift my spirit and restore my energy for the journey ahead. Help me rise with resilience and trust in the strength You provide. Amen.

Day 17 – Prayer for Discernment

Holy Spirit, sharpen my awareness of Your voice. Give me discernment to recognize truth, wisdom, and the right direction. Guide my choices so that my steps remain aligned with Your will. Amen.

Day 18 – Prayer for Release

Lord, I release every burden that has weighed upon my heart. Take what I cannot carry and replace it with Your sustaining grace. Let freedom rise in my spirit as I trust You completely. Amen.

Day 19 – Prayer for Healing

Great Healer, touch every wounded place within me. Restore what has been broken and renew my spirit with Your compassion. Let Your healing bring wholeness to my life. Amen.

Day 20 – Prayer for Vision

Lord, clarify the vision You have placed within my heart. Give me courage to write it, pursue it, and trust Your timing for its fulfillment. Guide my steps toward the future You are preparing. Amen.

Day 21 – Prayer for Rising

Lord, thank You for the journey of these twenty-one days. Continue shaping my life according to Your purpose and grace. Strengthen me to rise each day with wisdom, courage, and faith. Amen.

The 21 Rising Affirmations

A Daily Companion for Affirmation and Empowerment

Day 1 – I rise boldly into the new beginning God has prepared for me.

Day 2 – I rise unveiled and confident in the identity God has given me.

Day 3 – I rise awake, alive, and aligned with God's glory.

Day 4 – I rise centered, calm, and anchored in God's stillness.

Day 5 – I rise surrendered, strengthened, and safely held in God.

Day 6 – I rise confident, capable, and crowned with God's strength.

Day 7 – I rise grateful, grounded, and growing in God's goodness.

Day 8 – I rise aligned, guided, and moving in God's direction.

Day 9 – I rise courageous, bold, and upheld by God's strength.

Day 10 – I rise steady, secure, and anchored in God's faithfulness.

Day 11 – I rise filled with hope and divine expectation.

Day 12 – I rise wrapped in perfect peace.

Day 13 – I rise illuminated and guided by God's wisdom.

Day 14 – I rise strengthened by the joy of the Lord.

Day 15 – I rise favored and surrounded by God's goodness.

Day 16 – I rise renewed and strengthened by God.

Day 17 – I rise discerning and Spirit-led.

Day 18 – I rise free and unburdened.

Day 19 – I rise healing and whole.

Day 20 – I rise visionary and aligned with purpose.

Day 21 – I rise beautifully, boldly, and completely God's.

INSTITUTIONAL STRUCTURE

C² Educational Resource Center

Education • Leadership Development • Publishing • Consulting

C² Educational Resource Center serves as the foundational educational hub supporting publishing initiatives, leadership development, consulting programs, and educational resources.

Divisions

The Lady of Wisdom Publishing Company
Publishing and author development initiatives.

AI Momentum Consulting & Training
AI literacy, consulting, and strategic leadership training.

Educational Programs and Courses
Workshops, leadership development, and academic initiatives.

Independent Ministry

Tabernacle of Alpha & Omega
Tabernacle of Alpha & Omega operates as an independent nonprofit ministry dedicated to teaching, healing, and spiritual growth.

Academic Partnership

DCCJ Kingdom Theological Seminary
DCCJ Kingdom Theological Seminary provides theological education, leadership training, and ministry preparation.

Leadership

Founder & Visionary Leader
Dr. Carolyn Coleman
The Lady of Wisdom

About the Author

Dr. Carolyn Coleman, widely honored as The Lady of Wisdom, is an author, educator, counselor, pastor, and visionary leader whose work awakens purpose and healing in every life she touches.

As Founder and Bishop of Tabernacle of Alpha & Omega Church, and the creative force behind The Lady of Wisdom Publishing Company and DCCJ Kingdom Theological Seminary, Dr. Coleman equips believers to grow in identity, walk in purpose, and live with spiritual focus and emotional wholeness.

She is a prolific writer with devotionals, journals, anthologies, and educational curricula, who blends biblical truth with therapeutic insight, helping readers move from pain to power and from hesitation to holy becoming.

CONNECT WITH THE AUTHOR

Stay Connected with Dr. Carolyn Coleman

The Lady of Wisdom

Thank you for reading *Rise, Heal and Lead: A 21-Day Devotional for Women Called to Rise in Faith, Heal the Heart and Lead With God-Given Purpose.* If this devotional strengthened your faith, encouraged your healing, or inspired you to step forward in purpose, I invite you to stay connected. Through teaching, writing, mentoring, and leadership development, my mission is to help individuals grow in wisdom, faith, and spiritual clarity.

Website

Visit the official website for devotionals, resources, courses, and upcoming events:

DrCCTheLadyOfWisdom.com

Speaking and Training

Dr. Carolyn Coleman is available for:

- Women's Conferences
- Leadership Development Events
- Faith-Based Workshops
- Ministry Training
- Educational and Academic Engagements

For speaking inquiries and event bookings, please visit:

DrCCTheLadyOfWisdom.com

Educational and Leadership Development

Programs, training, and leadership initiatives are offered through:

C^2 Educational Resource Center

Providing resources in education, leadership development, consulting, and publishing.

Ministry

Dr. Carolyn Coleman serves as Founder of:

Tabernacle of Alpha & Omega

A Christ-centered ministry committed to teaching, spiritual growth, and community transformation.

Publishing

Books and devotionals by Dr. Carolyn Coleman are published through:

> The Lady of Wisdom Publishing Company

A Final Word

May you continue to rise in faith, heal in truth, and lead with wisdom.

Grace and peace,
Dr. Carolyn Coleman
The Lady of Wisdom

A Word to the Reader

Thank you for taking this 21-day journey through *Rise, Heal and Lead*.

My prayer is that these reflections helped you rediscover strength, embrace healing, and move forward with renewed courage and purpose. Every page was written with the hope that women everywhere would be reminded of the truth that they are called to rise, to heal, and to lead with wisdom.

If this devotional encouraged you, I invite you to consider sharing it with someone who may need the same encouragement.

Share the Journey

You may know a friend, sister, daughter, or colleague who would benefit from this message of faith and renewal. A simple recommendation can help another person begin their own journey of healing and purpose.

Leave a Review

If you found this devotional meaningful, your review can help other readers discover the book. Reviews help spread messages of encouragement and faith to readers who are searching for hope and guidance.

Stay Connected

For additional devotionals, resources, leadership teachings, and updates, please visit:

DrCCTheLadyOfWisdom.com

Continue Rising

Your journey does not end with the final page. Each day presents a new opportunity to rise in faith, heal in truth, and lead with courage.

May your path continue to unfold with wisdom, strength, and grace.

Dr. Carolyn Coleman
The Lady of Wisdom

www.ingramcontent.com/pod-product-compliance
Lightning Source LLC
Chambersburg PA
CBHW022056050726
47591CB00002B/567